The Nazi Death Camps

David Downing

WORLD ALMANAC® LIBRARY

Please visit our web site at: www.worldalmanaclibrary.com
For a free color catalog describing World Almanac® Library's list of
high-quality books and multimedia programs, call 1-800-848-2928 (USA)
or 1-800-387-3178 (Canada). World Almanac® Library's fax: (414) 332-3567.

Library of Congress Cataloging-in-Publication Data

Downing, David, 1946-
    The Nazi death camps / by David Downing.
      p. cm. — (World Almanac Library of the Holocaust)
    Includes bibliographical references and index.
    ISBN 0-8368-5947-2 (lib. bdg.)
    ISBN 0-8368-5954-5 (softcover)
    1. Holocaust, Jewish (1939-1945)—Juvenile literature. 2. World War, 1939-1945—
Concentration camps—Europe—Juvenile literature. 3. World War, 1939-1945—Jews—
Juvenile literature. I. Title. II. Series.
    D804.3.D69   2005
    940.53'18—dc22
                                                    2005040780

First published in 2006 by
World Almanac® Library
A Member of the WRC Media Family of Companies
330 West Olive Street, Suite 100
Milwaukee, WI 53212 USA

Produced by Discovery Books
Editors: Geoff Barker, Sabrina Crewe, and Jacqueline Gorman
Designer and page production: Sabine Beaupré
Photo researchers: Geoff Barker and Rachel Tisdale
Maps: Stefan Chabluk
Consultant: Ronald M. Smelser, Professor of Modern German History, University of Utah
World Almanac® Library editorial direction: Mark J. Sachner
World Almanac® Library editor: Alan Wachtel
World Almanac® Library art direction: Tammy West
World Almanac® Library production: Jessica Morris

Photo credits: cover: Corbis; title page: Topfoto.co.uk; p. 5: USHMM, courtesy of Instytut Pamieci
Narodowej; p. 6: Topfoto.co.uk; p. 8: ARCFI/www.deathcamps.org; p. 11: Topfoto.co.uk; p. 14:
Topfoto.co.uk; p. 15: Mary Evans PictureLibrary/Weimar Archive; p. 16: Hulton Archive/Getty Images;
p. 19: Mary Evans Picture Library/Weimar Archive; p. 20: ARCFI/www.deathcamps.org; p. 21: Topfoto.co.uk;
p. 22: USHMM, courtesy of Archiwum Dokumentacji Mechanicznej; p. 23: Topfoto.co.uk; p. 24:
Mary Evans Picture Library/Dr. David Lewis Hodgson; p. 26: Corbis; p. 29: Hulton Archive/Getty Images;
p. 30: Topfoto.co.uk; p. 32: Mary Evans Picture Library/Weimar Archive; p. 35: Mary Evans Picture Library/
Weimar Archive; p. 37: USHMM, courtesy of Instytut Pamieci Narodowej; p. 39: Michael St. Maur Sheil/
Corbis; p. 42: Bettmann/Corbis; p. 43: Mary Evans Picture Library/Weimar Archive.

Printed in Canada

1 2 3 4 5 6 7 8 9 09 08 07 06 05

Cover: This photograph shows a group of starving prisoners at the Ebensee concentration
camp in Austria. The picture was taken when the camp was liberated in May 1945.

Title page: This family was put to death in the Auschwitz death camp just after this photo was
taken. About one million people were murdered at Auschwitz in the years 1942 to 1944.

Contents

The Holocaust

The Murder of Millions

The word *holocaust* has a long history. In early times, it meant a burnt offering to the gods, and in the **Middle Ages**, a huge sacrifice or destruction. It still has this second meaning today, particularly when used to describe large-scale destruction by fire or nuclear weapons. But since the 1970s, the word has gained a new and specific meaning. Today, when people refer to the Holocaust—with a capital "H"—they mean the murder of approximately six million Jews by Nazi Germany and its **allies** during World War II.

This crime had deep historical roots. In predominantly Christian Europe, the Jews had always been considered a race apart and had often endured persecution for that reason. When governments or peoples wanted someone to blame for misfortune, they often picked on an innocent and helpless, Jewish minority.

In the early twentieth century, many Germans wanted someone to blame for their defeat in World War I and the terrible economic hardship that followed. They, too, picked on the Jews in their midst—with ultimately horrific results. The Holocaust was ordered and organized by political leaders, carried out by thousands of their willing supporters, and allowed to happen by millions of ordinary people.

The scale of the crime is still hard to take in. To use a modern comparison, about three thousand people were killed in the **terrorist** attacks in the United States on September 11, 2001. Between June 1941 and March 1945, an average of four thousand European Jews were murdered every day.

These people were killed in a variety of ways. Some were left to starve, some to freeze. Many were worked to death in **labor camps**. More than one million were shot and buried in mass graves. Several million were gassed to death in specially built **extermination camps** such as Auschwitz and Treblinka.

The Persecution of the Jews

The Jews were not the only victims of the Nazis. In fact, it is probable that the Nazis and their allies murdered at least five million other **civilians** before and during World War II. Their victims were killed for a variety of reasons: **communists** for their political opinions, **homosexuals** for their sexual orientation, people with mental disabilities for their supposed uselessness to society, **Gypsies** and Slavs for their supposed racial inferiority, and Russians, Poles, and other eastern Europeans because they happened to be in the Nazis' way.

The central crime in the Holocaust—the murder of millions of Jews—was a long time in the making. Most of the actual killing took place between 1941 and 1945, but Jews of Germany were subject to intense persecution from the moment Adolf Hitler and his Nazi Party took power in 1933. That persecution was itself merely the latest in a series of persecutions stretching back over almost two thousand years, in which every nation of Europe had at some time played a part.

This book looks at the camps that were specifically created as machines of mass murder. These **death camps** accounted for at least half of the victims of the Holocaust.

The sign above the gate and entrance to the main camp of Auschwitz (also called Auschwitz I) read "*Arbeit macht frei*" ("Work sets you free").

CHAPTER ONE

Building the Death Camps

Deciding on Genocide

By the autumn of 1941, the Nazis had already killed hundreds of thousands of Jews. Many had been randomly executed, and whole communities had been deliberately wiped out by starvation and disease in closely guarded **ghettos**. Thousands more people had been worked to death in labor camps, and nearly half a million had been shot by the ***Einsatzgruppen***, special **SS** units that followed the advancing German army as it invaded and occupied the Soviet Union. For Adolf Hitler and his fellow Nazis, however, even this flood of murder was too uncertain and too slow. At some point in the second half of 1941, Hitler is believed to have given the order to begin the systematic elimination of all Jews still living in German-occupied territory.

How was this to be done? According to SS leader Heinrich Himmler, the level of shootings in 1941 was already too stressful for his men, and that level would have to be greatly increased. The answer was murder by poisonous gas. This method was impersonal: It did not involve the one-on-one relationship between killer and victim that many of the killers found so upsetting. In addition, gas facilities could kill many more victims in the same amount of time.

Heinrich Himmler, leader of the SS, ordered and oversaw the murder of millions of people during World War II.

Chelmno and the Reinhard Camps

The Nazi authorities had been using poisonous gas as a weapon of mass murder for more than two years. Since September 1939, more than 70,000 Germans suffering from mental illness or other supposedly incurable conditions had been put to death in **gas chambers** and mobile gas vans at centers that were part of the **T-4 euthanasia program**. In the late fall of 1941, two of these vans were brought to the camp of Chelmno, some 40 miles (64 kilometers) north of Lodz in western Poland. They were then used in the mass murder of the 350,000 Jews still living in Warthegau, the name given to the section of Poland that had become part of the **Third Reich** (or the Reich, as the German regime was commonly called).

The gas vans operated by funneling carbon monoxide exhaust into the sealed back of the van. Obviously, each could

Heinrich Himmler (1900–1945)

Born in Bavaria, Heinrich Himmler attended a technical college and started work as a laboratory assistant before joining the Nazi Party in the early 1920s. He became head of the SS in 1929 and slowly turned it into the most powerful Nazi organization in Germany and, eventually, in German-occupied Europe. If Hitler's obsessive **anti-Semitism** was the driving force behind the Holocaust, Himmler was the faithful lieutenant who actually directed and oversaw it. He was the one who ordered the killing sprees of the *Einsatzgruppen* in the Soviet Union, and he supervised the creation of the death camps and gas chambers. Once the machinery of **genocide** was operating to his satisfaction, he did his best to keep it working both efficiently and secretly. Himmler was captured by the British in the final days of the war and committed suicide by swallowing a cyanide capsule.

murder only the number of people who could fit in the van. To make it possible to kill more people, the Nazis constructed stationary gas chambers with much greater capacity. These were built in the first half of 1942 at the camps of Belzec, Sobibor, and Treblinka in eastern Poland. All were in remote areas but close to railway lines. Diesel engines were used to fill the death chambers with carbon monoxide gas. Then the victims were buried in mass graves or burned in open pits. These three killing centers were eventually known as the "Reinhard Camps," after the SS leader Reinhard Heydrich, who had organized their construction before his assassination in May 1942. Between the spring of 1942 and the autumn of 1943, approximately 1.5 million Jews from Warsaw, Lublin, Lvov, and other Polish towns died in these gas chambers.

Majdanek and Auschwitz

Chelmno, Belzec, Sobibor, and Treblinka were "pure" death camps—that is, their only purpose was killing. The other two

An Engineer's Report

The SS had problems designing their gas vans. A large van could gas more people at one time, but the vehicle could become unstable. If they made the vans smaller, there were worries that the front axles would be over-loaded. An engineer was called in who assured the SS that this would not be the case. He reported, in chill-

ingly **dispassionate** terms, that "the balance is automatically restored, because the merchandise aboard displays during the operation a natural tendency to rush to the rear doors, and is mainly found lying there at the end of the operation. So the front axle is not overloaded."

This map shows the different Nazi camps in operation in 1942.

camps that are generally considered death camps are Auschwitz in southern Poland and Majdanek in eastern Poland. These were **concentration camps** that had been built earlier, to which gas chambers were added in 1942. They continued to operate as labor camps, however, and some Jewish arrivals at these camps were not killed immediately but added to the workforce.

The gas chambers in Majdanek, like those in the Reinhard Camps, used carbon monoxide. Those in Auschwitz, however, used a pesticide gas called Zyklon B. Experiments on Soviet prisoners of war in the fall of 1941 had shown that Zyklon B was easier to use and quicker to act than carbon monoxide, and the Auschwitz gas chambers were designed accordingly. To make it easier to dispose of the victims, each gas chamber was built beneath its own **crematorium** (for burning bodies).

Auschwitz was more efficient than the Reinhard Camps and outlasted them by more than one year. It seems probable that at least one million Jews perished in the gas chambers at Auschwitz.

CHAPTER TWO

Rounding Up the Victims

Getting Started

On January 20, 1942, a conference was held in the Berlin sub-
urb of Wannsee to discuss the **implementation** of Hitler's decision to begin the systematic elimination of Europe's Jews. The
minutes of that conference included a list of European nations
and their Jewish populations and announced that the continent
would be "combed through from west to east." The Nazis were
determined to make sure that no Jews escaped their net.

The Nazis had, of course, been rounding up Jews and
forcing them into virtual prisons since the beginning of World
War II, in September 1939. In Poland, and later in the occupied
territories of the Soviet Union, these prisons took the form of
closed ghettos. Most of the ghettos were only a short distance
from the newly built death camps. It was mostly people living
in the ghettos who were taken to the gas chambers through
the summer of 1942.

Roundups and Transit Camps

In the West, at first, it was only Jews born in Germany or
Poland who were rounded up and put in camps, like the one at
Gurs in southwestern France. Jews who had been born in the
West were subject to increasing persecution, but through 1941,
they remained mostly free. Then the situation changed. Once
the gas chambers were operating and the killing of the ghetto
Jews was well under way, strenuous efforts began to round up
Jews throughout the remainder of occupied Europe. In several
cities—including Paris, France; Amsterdam, the Netherlands;
and Athens, Greece—the authorities would pick out particular
areas, surround them with a ring of troops, and then scour
each street, house by house, for Jews. People captured in these
roundups were taken to **transit camps** or assembly camps

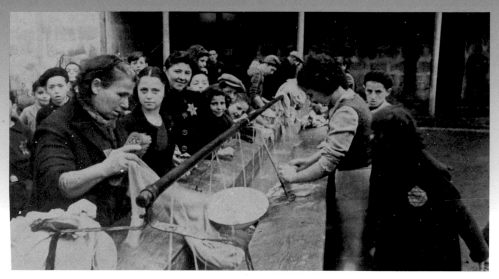

The washing facility at Drancy transit camp, northeast of Paris, in 1942. Most of the 73,000 French Jews rounded up by the French police were held in this camp before being shipped east to Auschwitz—and to their deaths.

(*Sammellager*), where they lived for days, weeks, or even months, until trains were available to move them on to the death camps.

Transit camps that became notorious were Drancy, on the outskirts of Paris, France, Malines in northern Belgium, and Westerbork in the northeast of the Netherlands. Some 150,000 Jews were sent east, mostly to Auschwitz, from these three camps. Only about 4,000 of them survived the war. Another infamous assembly point for prisoners was the Czechoslovakian ghetto at Terezin (called Theresienstadt by the Germans). About 142,000 Jews were brought there, half from Czechoslovakia, half from a wide range of other European countries. Of these people, 88,000 were sent to the death camps, 33,000 died in Theresienstadt itself, and about 20,000 somehow survived.

By 1944, the "combing" of Europe from west to east had been almost completed. Boats were bringing captured Jews from Norway to Germany, from Finland to Estonia, and from Aegean islands like Rhodes and Kos to the Greek mainland. Trains were moving Jews on from these ports and from transit camps in Lithuania, Italy, Hungary, Romania, Bulgaria, and the countries of the West. By this time, all lines led to Auschwitz.

Target List: The Nazi Estimate of Europe's Jewish Population in January 1942

The following list was presented to Nazi leaders at the Wannsee Conference in January 1942. Years later, historians noted that the second list—of nations not under direct German control—included some countries allied to Germany, some that were neutral, and some that were at war with Germany. In addition, some of the statistics were not accurate. For example, the figure for the Soviet Union was much too high because as many as one million of its Jews had already been murdered.

Nations or Areas Under Direct German Control	Number of Jews	Nations Not Under Direct German Control	Number of Jews
Germany (the Old Reich)	131,800	Bulgaria	48,000
Austria (renamed Ostmark)	43,700	England	330,000
Eastern territories	420,000	Finland	2,300
General Government (area of southeastern Poland)	2,284,000	Ireland	4,000
		Italy, including Sardinia	58,000
Bialystok	400,000	Albania	200
Protectorate of Bohemia and Moravia	74,200	Croatia	40,000
		Portugal	3,000
Estonia (free of Jews)	0	Romania, inc. Bessarabia	342,000
Latvia	3,500	Sweden	8,000
Lithuania	34,000	Switzerland	18,000
Belgium	43,000	Serbia	10,000
Denmark	5,600	Slovakia	88,000
Occupied France	165,000	Spain	6,000
Vichy France*	700,000	European Turkey	55,500
Greece	69,600	Hungary	742,800
Netherlands	160,800	Soviet Union**	5,000,000
Norway	1,300	** Includes 2,994,684 in Ukraine and 446,484 in Byelorussia.	

* Not occupied by Germany until November 1942 but in collaboration with the Germans throughout its existence.

TOTAL   **more than 11,000,000**

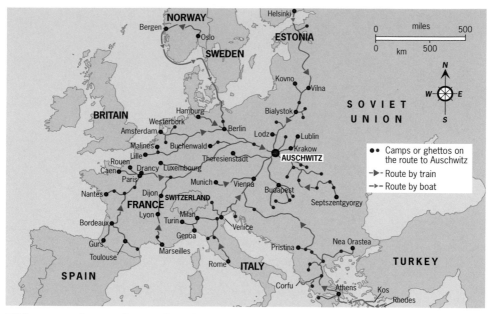

This map shows the major deportation routes to Auschwitz.

Helping and Hindering the Nazis

Some countries, and some peoples, were more helpful to the Nazis than others. Romanians carried out the first mass shooting of Jews in the Soviet Union. The *Einsatzgruppen* received significant help from people in the Ukraine, Lithuania, and Latvia, who identified Jews and served as auxiliary police and camp guards. In France, the **collaborationist** police, the *Milice Française*, rounded up Jews. In contrast, many other French people risked their lives to hide their Jewish **compatriots**.

Perhaps surprisingly, Nazi demands for the seizure and transportation of all Jews were most fiercely resisted by two of Germany's close allies, Italy and Hungary. The Italian leader Benito Mussolini thought Hitler's obsessive anti-Semitism was ridiculous. While he agreed publicly to transport Italy's Jews, Mussolini privately made it clear to his **subordinates** that they should do no such thing. His army generals in occupied Croatia and Albania made the same decision on their own.

The Hungarian dictator, Admiral Miklos Horthy, refused to round up and transport the 750,000 Jews living in Hungary. This inaction was more important than the Italians' as far as the Nazis were concerned. By the beginning of 1944, the Hungarian Jews formed by far the largest Jewish community

Dutch Jews board the train that will take them to a concentration camp.

Destination: Death

"At the railway station, we are split up in groups of 120 and more, and packaged into freight cars. The doors of the cars are shut. It is dark and tense, impossible to stretch your arms, absolutely no air to breathe. Everybody strangles and chokes and you feel as if a rope were tied around your neck and such a terrible heat, as if a fire had been set under the car.

"About ten people from our group are placed near the door; whoever has hairpins, nails, fasteners, starts to bore between the boards to get a little bit of air. People behind us are in much worse plight. . . . They are choking and driven unto the utmost despair.

"When, after a long waiting, the train is in motion, a sigh of relief emanates from the mouths of those who are still alive. They hope that now more air will find its way into the carriage, or it will start raining and a few drops will penetrate through the gaps. But none of these miracles happen. . . .

"I notice that in our carriage there is more and more free space. People die and we are seated on their dead bodies."

Zonka Pollak, a young Polish Jewish woman, describes a deportation journey on a train (from which she eventually escaped) in The Memorial Book of Chortzow, *edited by Yeshayahu Austri-Dunn, 1967*

supposedly within Hitler's grasp, and Horthy's refusal to let them go enraged Hitler. It was not until March 1944, when the German army occupied Hungary, that the SS were let loose on the country's Jews. Some 400,000 of them were eventually crammed into trains bound for Auschwitz.

Last Journeys

Those trains, like all the other trains that had transported Jews to their deaths over the previous two years, were characterized by the usual Nazi cruelty. Many of the journeys covered several hundred miles, and even the shorter ones—for example, the 300-mile (500-km) trip from Theresienstadt to Auschwitz—could take several days to complete. The conditions on board were horrible. There were no toilets, often not even buckets. Most of the cars were so crowded that it was impossible

A group of Dutch Jewish women stare out through the barbed wire bars of a train taking them east.

for anyone to lie down; this and the lack of adequate ventilation made it hard for most people to breathe. No food or water was provided. Not surprisingly, a large number of passengers died before they reached the death camps.

Those who died on the trains might have considered themselves lucky. Almost all of those that survived the journey— who waited, half-crazed with thirst, half-numb with fear, for the doors of the cattle cars to be flung open in Treblinka, or Belzec, or Sobibor—were about to die a terrifying death.

CHAPTER THREE

The Killing Process

Between the first regular gassings in Chelmno in December 1941 and the last gassings in Auschwitz in November 1944, a total of 3.5 million Jews arrived by train or truck at the six death camps. Because only partial records were kept, the exact figure will never be known. With only a few exceptions, those arriving in Belzec, Chelmno, Treblinka, or Sobibor were killed within hours. In Auschwitz and Majdanek, however, the need for workers in the adjoining mining and manufacturing operations meant that some new arrivals—about 25 percent of the men and 15 percent of the women—were selected to work and spared an immediate death. (Their fate is discussed in Chapter 4.)

The killing in Chelmno began several months before the stationary gas chambers became operational in the other five camps. Chelmno relied on the gas vans pioneered in the T-4 euthanasia program. The victims arrived by truck and were

New arrivals at Auschwitz: Jewish women and children wait for a Nazi committee to decide whether they will live or die. Most will go straight to the gas chambers.

taken inside a small villa known as "the Mansion." They were ordered to undress and then taken outside to a van, which they were told would take them to the bathhouse. The door of the van slammed shut, the driver started the engine, and the carbon monoxide exhaust was pumped into the back of the van, slowly killing those inside. Over the next fifteen minutes, the sounds of desperate struggles to break out slowly faded. Once silence fell, the van was driven into the nearby woods, where other prisoners had already dug a mass grave. These prisoners unloaded the van, carried the corpses to the grave, and waited for the van to return with a new load. At the end of each day, several of the gravediggers were shot, and replacements were chosen from the next day's arrivals at the Mansion.

Arrival

"We arrived around one o'clock in the morning in an area with lights, floodlights, and stench. We saw flames, tall chimneys. We still did not want to accept that it was Auschwitz. . . . The train stopped. Outside we heard all kinds of noises, stench, language, commands we didn't understand. Dogs barked. The doors flung open and we saw strange uniformed men in striped clothes. They started to yell at us in the **Yiddish** of Polish Jews: '*Schnell! Raus!*' ('Quick! Out!') We started to ask them, 'Where are we?' They answered, '*Raus, raus, raus!*' ('Out! Out! Out!') Sentries and their dogs were there, and they yelled at us also. '*Macht quick!*' ('Make it fast!')

"We got out and they told us to get in formations of five, and to leave all the luggage there. We asked one of the guys, 'Tell me, tell me, where are we going?' '*Dort, geht*' ('Over there'), and he pointed towards the flames."

*Alexander Ehrmann, who was in the first trainload of
Hungarian Jews to arrive at Auschwitz in 1944*

Knowing and Not Knowing

Those sent to the gas chambers at the other five camps had little time to realize their fate. Generally speaking, trains full of prisoners were sent only when there were gas chambers available; those who ran the camps did not want to deal with thousands of frightened Jews. It was much easier to keep things moving and give the victims as little time to think as possible. With this in mind, a wide range of measures were employed to trick the prisoners. Most arrivals had been told that they were being "resettled" and that they were going to be put to work. Many chose to hope that this was true, particularly in the early months of death camp operations. This hope became harder to sustain as growing numbers of rumors and eyewitness accounts emerged. The Nazis made great efforts to reassure their victims when they arrived. In Treblinka, for example, a pretend station was built, complete with signs to a ticket office and restaurant, and there were pots of flowers outside the gas chambers.

Death

"The door would now be quickly screwed up and the gas discharged by the waiting disinfectors through vents in the ceilings of the gas chambers, down a shaft that led to the floor. This insured the rapid distribution of the gas. It could be observed through the peepholes in the door that those who were standing nearest to the vents were killed at once. It can be said that about a third died straightaway. The remainder staggered about and began to scream and struggle for air. The screaming, however, soon changed to a death rattle and in a few minutes all lay still. . . . The door was opened half an hour after the introduction of the gas, and the ventilation switched on."

Rudolf Höss, camp commandant in Auschwitz,
describing the workings of the gas chambers

Perhaps some people were reassured and faced the dreadful truth only when the doors of the chambers slammed shut and the gas began to spread. Others knew all too well what was coming, but they tried to comfort their children and loved ones for as long as they could. It was hard to keep such hope alive when the stench of gas and burning bodies hung in the air.

The Gas Chambers

On arrival at the death camps (or after selection, in the case of Auschwitz and Majdanek), the condemned males and females were separated from each other, told to take off their clothes, and ordered to tie the laces of their shoes together. These shoes, their clothes, and any possessions they had managed to keep were then taken away. The women were marched into a large hut to have all their head and body hair cut off. While this was happening, the men were told that they were being taken for a shower. They were forced down a path or tunnel—lined with guards, barbed wire, or both—to the gas chamber. In Treblinka,

Women at Auschwitz, after being shaved. Their hair would be used, among other things, to make socks.

A local inhabitant and farmer, Kolodziejczyk, painted this impression of Belzec death camp. Unlike Auschwitz, the "pure" death camps had no need to house live prisoners and were quite small.

the guards called this passage the *Himmelfahrtstrasse,* or "Street to Heaven."

The "showers," windowless and lightless, usually held several hundred people. The men were crammed in, and the doors were sealed. In Belzec, Treblinka, Majdanek, and Sobibor, the motors began running and the carbon monoxide began flooding in. In Auschwitz, a few crystals of Zyklon B were dropped through vents in the roof, which were quickly slammed shut. By the time the men were all dead, the women were ready to follow them.

After Death

The dead bodies were hosed down and removed by teams of **Sonderkommando**—Jewish prisoners selected for this task. Gold teeth were extracted and dropped in buckets of acid to remove any flesh or bone. In Belzec and Sobibor, the corpses were burned in open pits; in Treblinka, they were at first buried in mass graves but later dug up and burned. The ashes were spread as fertilizer on the surrounding countryside. In Auschwitz, the bodies were taken on metal trolleys from the gas chambers to the elevators, which carried them up to the ovens of the crematoria. These ovens were rarely idle. During the murder of 400,000 Hungarian Jews in the summer of 1944, the chimneys grew so hot that the brickwork cracked and the lightning rods on top of them began to melt.

Victims of the gas chambers at Majdanek death camp were cremated in these ovens. Charred human remains can be seen on the ground.

The victims' possessions were sorted and, in many cases, sent to Germany to be redistributed among Germans. The clothes and the shoes, the letters and photographs, the crates of eyeglasses—all that remained of once prosperous lives after years of Nazi persecution and theft—were taken back on the trains that had brought their rightful owners to the camps. The gold teeth were melted down and made into gold bars. The hair of the women and girls was used to insulate submarine hulls and make socks for submarine crews.

The Holocaust of the Gypsies

The Gypsies, who include the Roma and Sinti peoples, were the other major ethnic group singled out by the Nazis for genocide. The Nuremberg Laws of 1935 called them an "alien strain" in Germany. In 1938–1939, most German Gypsies were sent to

the Buchenwald or Dachau concentration camps in Germany. (The Gypsies shown above were imprisoned at Belzec.) In 1940, those Gypsies who were still alive were moved to Poland, where special ghettos were created for them alongside the Jewish ghettos. In late 1941, transportation to Chelmno regularly included a Gypsy contingent, and within a few months, more than 4,300 had been murdered.

It seems unlikely that the Nazis ever made a decision to kill all of Europe's Gypsies. Generally speaking, settled communities of Gypsies were spared, while nomadic ones were killed. In the nations of Nazi-occupied Europe, the Gypsies met varying fates. In Bulgaria, Albania, and Slovakia, there was virtually no persecution; but in Romania, Yugoslavia, and Hungary, about 100,000 were murdered by the local authorities. The **Vichy government** in France (the government established after the German invasion) rounded up and deported some 30,000 Gypsies to the East, where almost two-thirds of them died. The genocide of the Gypsies is known as the *Porramous* ("Devouring"). Estimates of the total number killed in the *Porramous* vary greatly, but the figures generally fall between 0.25 and 0.5 million.

CHAPTER FOUR

Death Postponed

In Auschwitz and Majdanek, arrivals were lined up and inspected, usually by SS doctors. Those considered unfit for work—the old, the very young, and women with children—were waved in one direction, toward the gas chambers. The rest—mostly able-bodied adults between about sixteen and forty years old—were waved the other way. The Nazi war machine needed workers, so these few were spared, at least for the moment.

What horrors did these eyes witness? Prisoners stand behind a barbed-wire fence at Auschwitz.

Estimates vary, but of the 1.1 million Jews who arrived in Auschwitz, it appears that about 865,000 were sent straight to the gas chambers. The other 235,000 were used for slave labor. Of this group, some 110,000 remained in Auschwitz; about 100,000 of that number died there. The other 125,000 were sent on to other camps throughout Germany and Poland.

Processing at the Camps

Those spared on arrival were stunned by the fact that their families had just been torn apart, but they had little time to think about it. They were immediately processed by the camp authorities. Their possessions were taken away, and they were ordered to undress. Once they had been shaved all over, they were herded into the showers, supposedly to rid them of **lice**. They were then given their prison clothes, which looked like ragged, striped pajamas. The whole process was made as humiliating as possible. Sometimes the prisoners were left standing around naked for long periods, often in the hot sun or freezing cold. At other times, they were herded along by snarling dogs and men with clubs and whips. The showers were either icy or scalding; the camp clothes were full of lice and deliberately chosen to be too large or too small.

The prisoners then lined up to be registered. No records were kept of those sent immediately to the gas chambers, but those spared for work were each given a number. In most camps, this was sewn onto a uniform or worn around the wrist. In Auschwitz, the number was usually tattooed on an arm. Earlier arrivals at Auschwitz were photographed, but the vast number of people involved soon made that impractical.

A colored triangle sewn onto the prisoners' uniforms indicated the type of prisoner—a red triangle for political prisoners and priests, green for professional criminals, pink for homosexuals, brown for Gypsies, violet for **Jehovah's Witnesses**, and black for "a-socials" (such as alcoholics or prostitutes). Jews were given a black triangle as well as a yellow triangle. Sewn together, the two triangles formed a six-pointed **Star of David**.

A number was tattooed onto the arms of new arrivals who were selected for work rather than the gas chambers.

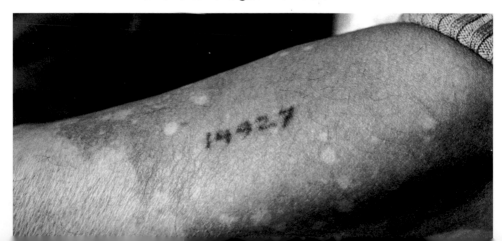

The First Days

The new arrivals spent their first few days in **quarantine** barracks. During this time, they were taught the rules of the camp and the need to obey any instruction instantly. Every morning they got up at about 4 A.M., made their beds, used the toilets, ate a minimal breakfast, and assembled outside in rows for the morning roll call. On some days, roll call lasted for hours; on others, the prisoners were given meaningless tasks to perform, like taking their caps on and off for hours on end. After evening roll call, they were fed and shut into their barracks until morning. Any mistake, any failure to do something perfectly, was instantly punished with a beating. Because the camp authorities were eager to keep the prisoners in a state of permanent terror, beatings were often handed out for no reason at all.

Once the quarantine period was over, the prisoners were moved into different barracks. The barracks themselves were

Roll Call

"A loud sound of a bell wakened everybody. All newcomers are quickly driven outside. We have to do exercises before the roll call. It is rather dark in the open and wet snow is falling. There is commotion in the camp, the numbers leave the barracks to attend the roll call. The cold is penetrating. One feels it through one's camp clothes. Bare feet soon begin to bother us. Shouts are heard, 'Fall into lines! Dress the ranks!' . . .

"At almost each block, beside the men standing in line, bodies of three, four persons are lying. These are the victims of the night that have not lived to see the day. Even yesterday they were standing numbers at the roll call and today they lie, lifeless and motionless. Life is not important at the roll call. Numbers are important. Numbers tally [must add up]."

Salmen Gradowski, a Polish Jew selected for labor at Auschwitz

Slave laborers lie in their barracks at Buchenwald concentration camp. This was not officially a death camp, but thousands died there from overwork, hunger, disease, and systematic violence.

stark and overcrowded, too hot in summer and freezing in winter, jammed with single bunks that were shared by three or more adults. A typical day's food consisted of watery turnip soup in the morning and bread that was mostly sawdust in the evening. Many died from starvation each day.

Starting Work

Once out of quarantine, prisoners began work. The hours of work were officially 6 A.M. to 5 P.M., with a half-hour break for food, but many prisoners worked much longer.

Auschwitz, in particular, offered a wide range of jobs, ranging from some that were survivable to others that were virtual death sentences. Auschwitz was actually three camps in one: the original concentration camp (called Auschwitz I), the Birkenau death camp (Auschwitz II), and the camp serving a giant I. G. Farben chemical and synthetic rubber-producing plant at Monowitz (Auschwitz III). Auschwitz I contained factories making arms and spare parts for three companies—Siemens, DAW, and Krupps. Nearby, there were coal mines, factories producing steel and shoes, a cement plant, and a center for defusing unexploded enemy bombs.

Death from Working

Many prisoners were killed by the work they were forced to do. The *Sonderkommando* who handled the dead bodies had the most inescapably fatal job in Auschwitz, because they were

The *Sonderkommando*

Jewish arrivals selected for immediate gassing were ushered to the chambers by a special unit of Jewish prisoners called the *Sonderkommando*. These men reassured the arrivals and kept up the pretense that they were on their way to take showers. In doing this, they both served the Nazi desire for minimum fuss and helped keep the victims' moments of terror as short as possible. Once the gas had done its work, it was the *Sonderkommando* who hosed the bodies down, pulled them from the chambers, and extracted their gold teeth. Then they piled the corpses into the ovens of the crematoria. Those who refused to serve as *Sonderkommando* were instantly executed, while those who agreed were given better food and living conditions until they themselves were murdered. Every few months, a new team of *Sonderkommando* was selected. The team's first job was to process and cremate its predecessors.

shot and replaced at regular intervals. Workers in the mines had an average life expectancy of one month; very few survived. At the I. G. Farben chemical plant, workers could expect to live three months, and 15,000 of the 40,000 employed there actually survived. A shoe factory was less likely to kill its workers than a chemical plant; an administrative job was a much healthier bet than physical labor. Perhaps the safest jobs were in the Auschwitz prisoners' orchestra, which played (non-Jewish) music for departing workers and arriving trains.

The assignment of work was, in many ways, a second selection process, with some prisoners pushed toward a probable death and others toward a much better chance of survival. In Auschwitz, Majdanek, and other camps, talents were evaluated differently than they had been in the outside world. Those with manual skills were in high demand and were allowed to use them. Those from academic or professional backgrounds had nothing the Nazis wanted, and they were likely to end up doing high-risk hard labor.

Slave Labor

"When we entered the women's barracks we were appalled. The scene before [us] was so horrifying that it didn't seem real. From the filthy yellow pallets, yellow-green ghouls looked out and in screeching voices invited us to draw near them. Yellow eyes peered out at us from all sides. . . . We were still dressed in coats and shoes, while they were wrapped in rags or paper with wooden clogs on their feet. We still looked young and fresh, while they looked old, bitter, gnawed to the bone by the yellow picric acid."

Maria Lewinger, remembering her arrival at the Skarzysko-Kamienna slave labor camp in Poland. The prisoners there used dangerous picric acid, which yellowed their skin, in the manufacturing of ammunition and explosives. Some 70 percent of the Jewish workers in the camp were shot when they became too weak to work.

A roll call for Polish prisoners takes place at Buchenwald concentration camp in 1943. These roll calls were often prolonged for hours in extreme temperatures.

Many Ways to Die

Each morning roll call had its dead, the bodies often propped up to be counted among the rows of living. These people had died in the night, some simply worn out by a combination of poor diet and overwork, some killed by the diseases that flourished in the unsanitary conditions. These were people, it should be remembered, who had been selected for their fitness to work.

When weakened by work and exhaustion, a prisoner was more likely to make mistakes, dropping a tool or not following

A mother and her small children, condemned to the gas chamber at Auschwitz, take their last walk.

an order quickly enough. Such mistakes almost always led to a beating or whipping, which weakened the prisoner even more. Some of the SS guards and commandants were **sadists** in any case, and several were clearly **psychopaths**. They shot people out of boredom, or for sport, or on a whim. There was no safe way for the prisoners to deal with such people.

Prisoners also faced the possibility that they would be chosen for the medical experiments carried out in Auschwitz and many other camps. In most cases, these were executions in all but name. The most infamous of the experimenters was Dr. Josef Mengele, who would stand by the arrival ramp at Auschwitz looking for suitable specimens among the incoming prisoners. He was particularly interested in twins, and they became the only children who were not sent to an immediate death. Other experiments were requested by drug companies such as Bayer, which wanted to test out new products for possible side effects. Like the twins, those prisoners who survived the experiments were usually gassed.

A Living Hell

It is almost impossible to describe the horror of a camp like Auschwitz. It was a place of death, instant or delayed, for so many totally innocent people. The initial selection condemned the vast majority to death and a sizable minority to a living hell. They lived and worked in conditions that were bound to weaken them, and weakness was a death sentence. Their original selection had not been a pardon, just a reprieve, a delay—and that reprieve could be revoked at any moment by a trigger-happy SS guard, a slip of the hand at a factory machine, or any demonstration of physical weakness. The prisoners had been selected because they were fit to work, and the moment that was no longer true, the selection was reversed. Then the prisoners were taken behind a building and shot or delivered to the line on the other side of the arrival ramp and pushed toward the gas chambers.

Girl in a Green Coat

"I watched a long column of trucks driving down the main road toward a red brick building about a thousand feet away. They were carrying Jews from Holland, someone told me. Young and old were standing up in the canvas-covered trucks. I particularly remember a girl with long blonde hair who was wearing a green . . . coat. 'Soon you will see the smoke; they are done for,' said the man next to me. And sure enough, the chimney started up. . . ."

Alfred Kantor, a Czech-Jewish prisoner in Auschwitz,
who later produced several paintings of the camp

CHAPTER FIVE

Those Responsible

The responsibility for the creation, operation, and long life of the death camps was widely shared. Some individuals ordered their establishment and decided the conditions under which they would operate. Others actually operated the camps, and some profited from their operation. And there were others, those who could have interfered with that operation but failed to do so.

Heinrich Himmler (front left) inspects Auschwitz III (also known as Monowitz) with SS officers and engineers from the I. G. Farben chemical company in July 1942.

The Instigators

As far as is known, Adolf Hitler never set foot anywhere near a death camp, but the camps were inspired by his determination to exterminate the Jews, and it was he who gave the order for their creation. His closest political colleagues, including Joseph Goebbels and Hermann Göring, were enthusiastic supporters of the genocide.

As leader of the SS, Heinrich Himmler was responsible for the actual operation of the death camps. He visited Auschwitz, watched the killing process at work, and pronounced himself satisfied. Theodore Eicke, Himmler's inspector of concentration camps until 1939, set the tone for official behavior, lecturing the commandants and guards on the need to ignore any feelings of pity. They should never forget, he told them, that

Rudolf Höss (1900–1947)

After serving as a soldier in World War I, Rudolf Höss joined the right-wing *Freikorps*. He was sent to prison for murdering a man he claimed was a traitor to Germany, but he was released in 1928. Höss joined the SS in 1934 and worked in the Dachau and Sachsenhausen concentration camps in Germany for the next six years. In 1940, he became commandant of Auschwitz, organizing the experimental use of Zyklon B on Soviet prisoners of war in 1941 and setting up Auschwitz II as a death camp in 1942. During the final two years of the war, he was deputy inspector general of the entire concentration camp system. Höss evaded capture for a while after the war but was hanged by the Polish authorities at the site of Auschwitz in 1947. Talking about his time as commandant of Auschwitz, Höss recalled that his wife's garden there was "a paradise of flowers" and that his five children loved to splash around in their wading pool. "I am completely normal," he wrote in his autobiography. "I led a completely normal life."

their emblem was the Death's Head (a skull) and that they each carried a loaded gun.

The Human Tools

The Nazis established **hierarchies** in the camps themselves. The camp commandants, who were in charge, usually lived in ordinary-looking houses just outside the camp, often with their wives and children. They ate well, entertained their fellow officers, and tried to ignore the smells of gas and corpses that wafted in through their windows. After the war, some of the camp commandants unsuccessfully tried to argue that they had only been figureheads without power and that others had really run the camps. They all appeared to lack a sense of right and wrong.

SS guards and their officers ran the day-to-day business of the camps. There were about 24,000 SS in mid-1944, most working in labor or concentration camps. Auschwitz employed about 7,000 guards during its existence, about 3,000 at any one time. In general, the guards had an easy life. They were well-fed, lived in reasonable conditions, and—unlike their colleagues serving in the field—were extremely unlikely to face an armed enemy.

Minute-by-minute supervision was left to specially selected prisoners, called *Kapos* in the case of those who supervised work teams and *Blockältesters* in the case of those in charge of barracks. Most were non-Jewish German criminals who had been chosen for their love of violence, but some of them tried to help the prisoners they supervised. They had their own rooms in the barracks and better food, but like everyone else in the camps, they were ultimately at the mercy of the SS.

Profiting Businesses

A number of different businesses profited from the operation of the death and concentration camps. Topf & Sons of Erfurt, for example, designed and installed the crematorium ovens at Auschwitz as if it was the sort of business order the company received every day. And I. G. Farben, the chemical company,

Dachau prisoners provided plentiful, cheap labor at the concentration camp's munitions factory.

saw no reason to turn down hugely increased orders for the poisonous crystals Zyklon B.

The theft of clothes, possessions, and even hair from arriving prisoners was a profitable business for SS camp officers, but they made even more money hiring out the prisoners who were not immediately put to death. The workers supplied by the death, concentration, and labor camps came cheap. The I. G. Farben chemical plant in Auschwitz III paid the SS the sum of $1 a day for each skilled worker, 75¢ for each unskilled workers, and 40¢ for each child worker. The workers, of course, received nothing. Many other businesses profited from using camp prisoners. Fifty-one companies used slave labor supplied by the Auschwitz camps, including the German subsidiary of the Ford Motor Company.

Turning a Blind Eye

Who could have brought the operation of the death camps to a halt? In occupied Europe, only one group had the power to stop the genocide—the men who commanded the German army. They chose not to do so. Some were committed Nazis and anti-Semites, but most were not. As the extent of the Holocaust became apparent during 1942 and 1943, they looked the other way. A small group of German officers tried to assassinate Hitler in July 1944, but they were motivated by fears for their country, not by concern for the Jews.

Other European governments had some power to delay the delivery of Jews to the Nazi killing machine. A few of them— the Hungarian and Italian governments, in particular—took

Failure to Act

In the early summer of 1944, news reached London and Washington, D.C., of the mass murder of the Hungarian Jews shipped to Auschwitz. The Jewish rescue organizations that had brought this news begged the Allies to do something that would stop the murder machine in its tracks. They suggested bombing the gas chambers and the railroad lines that supplied the camps. British prime minister Winston Churchill told his staff to organize something along these lines, but they took no action, stressing the military difficulties involved and the need for the United States to agree to any bombings. The United States did not approve the move. It said Allied bombers should carry on with the job they were doing: hitting German industry and weakening Germany's will to fight on. By 1944, when the possibility of bombing the camps arose, it was too late to save the majority of the Jews killed, but the Allies' failure to bomb Auschwitz may have cost Jewish lives in the last year of the war.

This view shows Auschwitz I after liberation in 1945. The long building beyond the electrified fence houses the camp's kitchens.

advantage of that power and undoubtedly saved many lives as a result. Other governments, such as the Vichy government in France, did everything the Nazis asked and sometimes more.

Finally, there were the governments of the nations at war with Germany. The first rumors of the death camps in these countries were not believed; many people remembered stories of German atrocities during World War I that had turned out to be untrue. It soon became clear, however, that something terrible really was happening. What should the Allies do? They decided to stick with their **blockade** of the European continent and with their refusal to negotiate with the Nazi regime. The alternative—to relax the blockade and attempt to make a deal with Hitler to save at least some Jews—was not acceptable. The only sure way to help the Jews, the Allies said, was to win an unconditional surrender. Unfortunately, by the time the war was won, most of Europe's Jews were beyond help.

CHAPTER SIX

Running Out of Time

The Gassing Ends

When the death camps were established in 1942, the German army was still advancing in the Soviet Union and North Africa. Following defeats at El Alamein in northern Egypt in late 1942 and at Stalingrad in the Soviet Union in early 1943, Germany moved onto the defensive. By mid-1943, many Germans had realized that the war was likely to end in their defeat. By mid-1944, the Soviet Red Army's advance into eastern Europe as well as the British and U.S. invasion of France had made Germany's defeat certain. It was not, however, the approach of the Red Army that caused the Nazis to close Chelmno and the Reinhard Camps (Belzec, Sobibor, and Treblinka). They were shut down during 1943 because they had finished the job for which they had been created—the murder of Poland's Jews.

This left Majdanek and Auschwitz to complete the killing of the remaining European Jews. Majdanek, farther east, was abandoned in the summer of 1944, but the killing at Auschwitz continued in record numbers throughout that summer and fall. As defeat loomed, Hitler's priority became crystal clear: to kill as many more Jews as possible. Railroad vehicles and lines that were badly needed by the German army were given to the SS for the transportation of the Hungarian Jews to Auschwitz. It was only in November 1944 that the approach of the Red Army forced Himmler to end the gassing and abandon the Auschwitz complex.

Destroying the Evidence

The Nazi authorities, although privately proud of their bold approach to the "Jewish problem," were fully aware that the rest of the world considered genocide a crime without parallel.

They had always been careful to conceal the existence of the death camps. From the beginning, they used code words to describe their operations. Deportation to a death camp was called "resettlement," and killing was called "special action" or "special measures." Hardly anything was put in writing. As Himmler told a group of SS leaders in October 1943, the annihilation of the Jewish people was being conducted in a "tactful" silence. It would, he went on, be "an unwritten and never-to-be-written page of glory" in SS history.

To make sure of this, he ordered the complete destruction of the death camps. In the cases of Chelmno and the Reinhard Camps, there was plenty of time to carry this out, and all traces of the killing process at these sites were destroyed. At Auschwitz and Majdanek, more speed was needed, and the demolition was not quite as thorough. Some records were recovered, along with vast stores of prisoners' belongings that had not been destroyed or sent to Germany. At Auschwitz, for example, the Red Army found 38,000 pairs of shoes.

A roomful of shoes was discovered at the abandoned Auschwitz. The SS had not had time to destroy this evidence of thousands of murders.

The Death Marches

As the Red Army advanced toward the German heartland in the final months of the war, the SS carried out a final selection of the surviving inhabitants of the death, concentration, and labor camps in Poland and eastern Germany. Those considered too weak to travel or work were abandoned or killed, while the rest were sent to camps further west. Sometimes there were trains or trucks available for transportation, but often the poorly dressed prisoners were forced to walk hundreds of miles through the harsh eastern European winter weather. Already

On the March

"We were lined up in rows of five and told that we will have to walk, and that anybody trying to escape will be shot. It was very cold and snowing.

"We went westward walking in our wooden shoes on icy snow-covered roads. We were still in our striped thin clothes. Many collapsed and they were immediately shot on the spot. We had to take the corpses and throw them into a ditch next to the road. The SS surrounded each of our columns and were ready with their guns.

"After walking the whole day and part of the night, we reached a brick factory where we were allowed to rest and sleep under cover. Only half of us were still alive when we reached the factory. One in our group, a French political prisoner, did not wake up. He was dead, frozen stiff. I took his red triangle from his tunic, put it in my pocket, hoping to exchange it later for my Star of David insignia. Finally we were taken to a railway station and squeezed into an open cattle wagon, standing room only. We thus traveled through Austria and Germany seven days and seven nights until we reached our destination. Nine in our wagon died during the journey."

Freddie Knoller, an Austrian Jew evacuated from Auschwitz
as the Red Army approached in 1945

This map shows the routes of the "death marches" to camps further west that took place during the final months of World War II.

weakened by hunger and ill-treatment, many people found it impossible to continue. They were shot where they fell. About 100,000 Jews died on these "death marches."

The "Dying Camps"

Those who reached their new camps were at first put to work. They built defenses, constructed underground factories for new secret weapons, and did any of the numerous jobs needed to keep the German armed forces fighting. As defeat grew nearer and the Reich slowly shrank toward nothing, however, the will and ability of the SS to organize its victims broke down. The SS's final means of murder was death by neglect. In so-called "dying camps," the Jews and other surviving enemies of the Reich were simply dumped behind barbed wire without food or water and left to die. Bergen-Belsen, in Germany, was the most notorious of these camps. In late 1944, it became a dumping ground for Jews evacuated from all over the East, including 10,000 survivors from Auschwitz. Through the last months of

41

the war, inmates died each night from starvation, thirst, or disease. Their bodies were simply piled in front of the barracks.

Liberation

Liberation of the camps by Allied troops in 1945 came too late for many prisoners. When the British reached Bergen-Belsen, they found piles of skeletal remains and thousands of gaunt, starved survivors, many too weak to speak or move. In April 1945, when British and U.S. forces entered Buchenwald, Dachau, Sachsenhausen, Ravensbrück, Mauthausen, and many other smaller camps, they encountered similar scenes of horror and inhumanity. Appalled and enraged by what they saw, many Allied commanders brought German civilians from nearby towns and villages out to the camps and forced them to look at what had been done in their name.

On April 30, 1945—only days before World War II ended in Europe—Hitler killed himself in his Berlin bunker. The previous day, he had written a political testament in which

Under orders from the British liberators of Bergen-Belsen, female Nazi guards fill a mass grave with the bodies of the camp's former inmates.

Liberation: Dachau is freed by U.S. troops in April 1945. About 33,000 survivors were found, but thousands had died in the preceding weeks.

he placed the blame for World War II squarely on the Jews. He wrote that the Jews had paid for their alleged guilt, however, "by more humane means than war." Hitler, unbelievably, was referring to the gas chambers of the death camps, which had consumed at least three million Jewish lives.

Left to Die

"I picked my way over corpse after corpse in the gloom until I heard one voice. I found a girl, she was a living skeleton, impossible to gauge her age for she had practically no hair left, and her face was only a yellow parchment sheet with two holes in it for eyes. She was . . . trying to cry but she hadn't enough strength. And beyond her down the passage and in the hut there were the convulsive movements of dying people too weak to raise themselves from the floor."

BBC correspondent Richard Dimbleby,
reporting from Bergen-Belsen on April 19, 1945

Time Line

1929 Heinrich Himmler becomes leader of the SS.

1933 Nazi Party comes to power in Germany.

1935 Nuremberg Laws legalize persecution of Jews, Gypsies, and others in Germany.

1938–1939 German Gypsies are sent to Dachau and Buchenwald.

1939 September: German attack on Poland begins World War II.

1939–1941 70,000 Germans with "incurable" diseases and conditions are killed under T-4 euthanasia program.

1940 German Gypsies are moved to ghettos in Poland.
Rudolf Höss becomes commandant of Auschwitz.

1941 June: Germany invades Soviet Union.
July: Mass shootings of Soviet Jews by *Einsatzgruppen*.
September: Zyklon B gas tested on Soviet prisoners of war; Nazis decide to kill all of Europe's Jews.
December: Gas vans begin regular operations at Chelmno.

1942 January 20: Wannsee Conference is held in Berlin.
March: Death camp at Belzec opens, followed in the next months by the opening of death camps at Sobibor and Treblinka.
April: Gas chambers open at Auschwitz, followed by the opening of gas chambers at Majdanek in November.
December: SS decree orders the sending of Gypsies to Auschwitz.

1943 January–October: Chelmno, Belzec, Treblinka, and Sobibor are shut down.

1944 March: Germany occupies Hungary; transportation of Hungarian Jews to Auschwitz soon follows.
May: News of mass killings at Auschwitz reaches the West; pleas to bomb Auschwitz are rejected by Winston Churchill and Franklin D. Roosevelt.
July: Group of German army officers fails in attempt to kill Adolf Hitler.
Summer: Majdanek is abandoned. "Death marches" of prisoners to the West begin.
November: Auschwitz is abandoned.

1945 April: Dachau, Buchenwald, Bergen-Belsen, and other camps are liberated by western Allies.
April 30: Hitler commits suicide.
May: World War II ends in Europe.

Glossary

allies: people, groups, or nations that agree to support and defend each other. "The Allies" were the nations that fought together against Germany in World War I and World War II.

anti-Semitism: prejudice against Jews.

blockade: setting up of obstruction to prevent goods entering or leaving a particular region.

Blockältester: prisoner placed in charge of barracks in a prison camp.

civilian: person who is not serving in the military.

collaborationist: helping an invading or occupying power.

communist: person who believes in the principles of communism, a political system in which government owns and runs the nation's economy. (A Communist with a capital "C" is a member of the Communist Party.)

compatriot: person belonging to the same nation as another person.

concentration camp: prison camp set up by the Nazis to hold Jews and other victims of the Nazi regime. Many prisoners held in these camps were never tried or given a date of release.

crematorium: building in which bodies are burned.

death camp: another term for extermination camp.

dispassionate: not showing personal feelings.

Einsatzgruppen: special SS units operating behind the advancing German army and ordered to murder Jews and other enemies of the Nazis.

extermination camp: place set up by Nazis in which they murdered large numbers of people.

gas chamber: airtight room or other space in which people are gassed to death.

genocide: deliberate murder or attempted murder of a whole people.

ghetto: usually poor and overcrowded part of a city, occupied by a minority group because of social, legal, or economic pressure.

Gypsy: member of a group that includes the Roma and Sinti peoples, who live mostly in Europe. Gypsies are traditionally nomadic, meaning they move from place to place.

hierarchy: grading or ranking of individuals.

homosexual: person attracted to others of the same sex.

implementation: putting into effect.

Jehovah's Witness: member of a Christian sect that believes in the imminent end of life. Jehovah's Witnesses have traditionally believed their own principles more important than obedience to political authority.

Kapo: prisoner placed in charge of work teams in prison camps.

labor camp: camp in which prisoners are forced to perform hard labor.

lice: insects that infest human hair and skin.

Middle Ages: period of European history from about A.D. 500 to 1500.

psychopath: person suffering from a mental disorder involving antisocial behavior.

quarantine: period of isolation, usually to prevent the spread of disease.

sadist: person who enjoys being cruel to others.

Sonderkommando: Jewish prisoners in death camps who dealt with the bodies of those who were murdered.

SS: short for *Schutzstaffel*, a Nazi elite force also known as "the blackshirts."

Star of David: six-pointed star that is the emblem of the Jewish people.

subordinate: belonging to a lower rank.

T-4 euthanasia program: Nazi program that undertook deliberate killing of people with supposedly incurable conditions or diseases.

terrorist: person who performs acts of violence in order to make a political point or force a change in government policy.

Third Reich: name given by the Nazis to their regime. The name means "third empire," following the First Reich (the medieval Holy Roman Empire) and the Second Reich (1870–1918).

transit camp: camp where people are kept prior to being moved elsewhere.

Vichy government: French government set up in 1940 to administer the area of France not under direct German occupation.

Yiddish: language of the Jews in eastern Europe that includes elements of Hebrew, German, and Slavic languages.

Further Resources

Books

Altman, Linda Jacobs. *Hitler's Rise to Power and the Holocaust* (The Holocaust in History). Enslow Publishers, 2003.

Byers, Ann. *The Holocaust Camps* (Holocaust Remembered). Enslow Publishers, 1998.

Saldinger, Anne Grenn. *Life in a Nazi Concentration Camp* (The Way People Live). Lucent Books, 2000.

Sheehan, Sean. *The Death Camps* (Holocaust). Raintree, 2001.

Shuter, Jane. *Auschwitz* (Visiting the Past). Heinemann Library, 2000.

Shuter, Jane. *Life and Death in the Camps* (The Holocaust). Heinemann Educational Books, 2002.

Web Sites

The Holocaust: Crimes, Heroes and Villains
www.auschwitz.dk
Web site about those involved in the Holocaust, with biographies, poetry, photos, and more.

The Holocaust History Project
www.holocaust-history.org
Archive of documents, photos, and essays on various aspects of the Holocaust.

Holocaust Survivors
www.holocaustsurvivors.org
Interviews, photos, and sound recordings of survivors of the Holocaust.

The Museum of Tolerance's Multimedia Learning Site
motlc.wiesenthal.org
Educational Web site of the Simon Wiesenthal Center, a Jewish human rights agency.

Non-Jewish Holocaust Victims
www.holocaustforgotten.com
A site dedicated to the Nazis' five million non-Jewish victims.

United States Holocaust Memorial Museum
www.ushmm.org
Personal histories, photo archives, and museum exhibits of the Holocaust.

About the Author

David Downing has been writing books for adults and children about political, military, and cultural history for thirty years. He lives in Britain.

Index